First World War
and Army of Occupation
War Diary
France, Belgium and Germany

59 DIVISION
178 Infantry Brigade
Sherwood Foresters
(Nottinghamshire and Derbyshire Regiment)
2/7th Battalion
14 September 1914 - 28 February 1916

WO95/3025/5

The Naval & Military Press Ltd
www.nmarchive.com
Published in association with The National Archives

Published by

The Naval & Military Press Ltd

Unit 10 Ridgewood Industrial Park,

Uckfield, East Sussex,

TN22 5QE England

Tel: +44 (0) 1825 749494

www.naval-military-press.com

www.nmarchive.com

This diary has been reprinted in facsimile from the original. Any imperfections are inevitably reproduced and the quality may fall short of modern type and cartographic standards.

© **Crown Copyright**
Images reproduced by permission of The National Archives, London, England, 2015.

Contents

Document type	Place/Title	Date From	Date To
Heading	WO 3025 59 Div 178 Inf Br 2/7 Bn Sherwood Foresters 1914 Sep-1916 Feb		
Heading	59 Division 178 Inf Brigade 2/7 Bn Sherwood Foresters 1914 Sep-1916 Feb		
Heading	War Diaries Of 2/7th Sherwood Foresters September To December 1914		
War Diary	Nottingham	14/09/1914	28/11/1914
Miscellaneous	Statement Attached To War Diary 2/7th Battalion Sherwood Foresters		
War Diary	Nottingham	01/12/1914	26/12/1914
Miscellaneous	Statement Attached To War Diary Of December 1914 Of 2/7th Sherwood Foresters		
Heading	War Diaries Of 2/7th Sherwood Foresters January To April and September To December 1915		
Miscellaneous	British Salonika Force War Diary		
War Diary	Nottingham	02/01/1915	31/01/1915
Miscellaneous	Statement For Jan. 1915 2/7th Sherwood Foresters		
War Diary	Tuten	01/02/1915	05/02/1915
War Diary	Ongar	08/02/1915	24/02/1915
Miscellaneous	2/7th Sherwood Foresters Statement With War Diary February 1915		
War Diary	Luton	02/03/1915	30/03/1915
Miscellaneous	2/7th Sherwood Foresters Statement With War Diary March 1915		
War Diary	Luton	01/04/1915	30/04/1915
Miscellaneous	2/7th Sherwood Foresters Statement With War Diary April 1915		
War Diary	Watford	02/09/1915	30/11/1915
Miscellaneous	Statement Attached To War Diary For November		
War Diary	Watford	02/12/1915	31/12/1915
Miscellaneous	Statement Attached To War Diary For December 1915		
Miscellaneous	From O.C. 2/7th Sherwood Foresters	16/12/1915	16/12/1915
Miscellaneous	178th Infantry Brigade	27/10/1915	27/10/1915
Miscellaneous	War Diary	15/12/1915	15/12/1915
Heading	War Diary Of 2/7th Batt. Sherwood Foresters From 1st To 31st January 1916		
War Diary	Watford	05/01/1916	31/01/1916
Miscellaneous	2/7th Sherwood Foresters Statement With War Diary Jan 1916		
Heading	War Diary Of 2/7th Sherwood Foresters From Feb 1st 1916 To Feb 29th 1916 (Vol XVII)		
War Diary	Watford	02/02/1916	28/02/1916
Miscellaneous	2/7th Battalion The Sherwood Foresters	28/02/1916	28/02/1916

WO 3025

59 DIV 178 INF BR

2/7 BN SHERWOOD FORESTERS

1914 Sep — 1916 Feb

59 DIVISION

178 INF BRIGADE

2/7 BN SHERWOOD FORESTERS

1914 SEP — 1916 FEB

War Diaries of
2/7th Sherwood Foresters.

September to December
1914.

Army Form C. 2118

WAR DIARY
or
INTELLIGENCE-SUMMARY
(Erase heading not required.)

2/7th Battn Sherwood Foresters.

Instructions regarding War Diaries and Intelligence Summaries are contained in F.S. Regs., Part II. and the Staff Manual respectively. Title Pages will be prepared in manuscript.

Place	Date	Hour	Summary of Events and Information	Remarks and references to Appendices
	1914.			
NOTTINGHAM	Sept. 14th		First Recruit Enlisted. Major P.M.Payne detailed to Command the Battalion.	
	19th		Strength - 221 All Ranks.	
	26th		" - 229 "	
	Oct. 4th		" - 433 "	
	10th		" - 507 "	
	17th		" - 596 "	
	20th		30 men were sent to ~~Booking, Essex~~ Magendon, to join the 1/7th Battalion Sherwood Foresters as ~~First~~ a draft to replace Home Service men who had gone to the Reserve Battalion at Dunstable reinforcements. These men had not fired a Course of Musketry and were mere recruits.	
	24th		Strength - 666 All Ranks.	
	31st		" - 12 Officers 786 N.C.O's and Men.	

P.M.Payne
Major
Commanding 2/7th Sherwood Foresters

Army Form C. 2118

Instructions regarding War Diaries and Intelligence
Summaries are contained in F.S. Regs., Part II.
and the Staff Manual respectively. Title Pages
will be prepared in manuscript.

WAR DIARY
or
INTELLIGENCE SUMMARY

(Erase heading not required.)

2/7th Sherwood Foresters.

Place	Date	Hour	Summary of Events and Information	Remarks and references to Appendices
NOTTINGHAM.	Sept. & October 1914.		(1) ACCOMMODATION. From the date of the formation of the Battalion, men were living in their own homes. They were paid 2/- per diem subsistance allowance. It was found that this system was subversive of discipline, because men lived at great distances apart and adequate supervision was impossible. (2) CLOTHING. Men were not immediately provided with uniform. During the months in question they paraded in Civilian clothes, which was no doubt a detriment to recruiting. In November of the same year clothing was supplied by the Territorial Force Association. (3) NUMBERS. 227 men were enlisted during September and 562 during October. No unfit men were sent from the First Line. (4) RECRUITING. Recruiting for the Territorial Force was done separately from that of the Regular Army, and they did not clash. The organisation of a Band at the very start would have aided recruiting. A great many men were rejected for height or chest measurement, who were otherwise physically sound. (5) MEDICAL SERVICE. Recruits were examined by Civilian Doctors who passed a considerable number of men who were not fit for the Army. Their chief defects were Visual and Dental. In my opinion these men were passed inadvertently and not for purpose of gain. (6) KIT & EQUIPMENT. In my opinion, the issue of a full kit and equipment on Attestation would have been an inducement to join men to join. (7) SANITATION. During the months in question, the men being in their own homes, there was no difficulty as to Latrine accommodation. (8) DISCIPLINE. N.C.O's were made straight from the ranks, from among the recruits, with the result that their authority was not as strong as it ought to have been. I should recommend that in forming a Reserve Battalion, a considerable number of experienced Non-Commissioned Officers should be transferred to it from the Service Battalion in order to ensure a sufficiently high standard of discipline from the start.	

L. M. Payne
Major
Commanding 2/7 Sherwood Foresters.

Army Form C. 2118

WAR DIARY
or
INTELLIGENCE SUMMARY 2/7 Sherwood Foresters
(Erase heading not required.)

Instructions regarding War Diaries and Intelligence Summaries are contained in F.S. Regs., Part II. and the Staff Manual respectively. Title Pages will be prepared in manuscript.

Place	Date	Hour	Summary of Events and Information	Remarks and references to Appendices
Nottingham	Nov 1914			
	1st		Strength Officers 12. O.Ranks 788.	
	7th		" " 12 " 893	
	10th		2 Officers and 119 2COS men were sent to Harpenden as 1st reinforcements to the 1/7th Sherwood Foresters. The majority of these men had been previously served with as regulars or territorials, but had none of them had previously a months service prior to them battalion.	
	14th		Strength Officers 12. O.Ranks 902	
	21st		" " 12 " " 902	
	28th		" " 12 " " 905	

S. N. Sayn
Major

Statement attached to
War Diary 2/7th Battalion Sherwood
Foresters
November 1914.

1. **Training**
    The training received during the month consisted of Squad drill with and without arms, Company drill and route marching.

2. **Billets**
    Officers and men were living for the most part in their own homes receiving 2/- per day subsistence allowance: the few whose homes were at a distance were billeted at the 9d rate, drawing 1/9 per day ration allowance.

3. **Parades**
    The hours of parade were 8.45 am - 1 pm and 2.30 pm - 5 pm. Instructional classes for Officers and NCOs were held from 6-7 pm three days per week: Officers under a colour sergeant Instructor, NCOS under the Battalion Sergeant Major.

4. **Music**
    A good bugle band was started, which played the Battalion to its training ground daily

5. **Training Grounds**
    On searching for training grounds with a view to simple tactical exercises, there was considerable difficulty in obtaining the use of suitable land close at hand. I should suggest that in such circumstances more power to use land where clearly no damage would be done ought to be given to Officers commanding and training new battalions.

6. **Discipline**
    Men living in their homes, scattered at distances from Headquarters was not satisfactory: also the lack of experienced

non commissioned officers was a drawback

7. Medical Service

The civilian medical practitioner who had been appointed held a sick parade each morning. He also examined the men who presented themselves for enlistment. The class of men passed and enlisted at this time was up to the average for the regular army.

J. M. Payne
Major

WAR DIARY or INTELLIGENCE SUMMARY

Army Form C. 2118

2/7 Sherwood Foresters

Place	Date	Hour	Summary of Events and Information	Remarks and references to Appendices
Retford	1914 Dec			
	1st		Strength 12 officers 905 other ranks.	
	2nd		" 16 " 904 "	
	3rd		" 17 " 975 "	
	13th		20 NCOs and men were sent to Bakery as a draft to the 1/7th Sherwood Foresters. These men have been previous service, but have not been a course of musketry since joining this battalion.	
	19th		Strength 18 officers 1001 other ranks.	
	26th		Strength 18 " 1000 "	

P.M. Payne
Major

Statement attached to War Diary
of December 1914 of
2/7th Sherwood Foresters.

1. Training

Simple tactical exercises were undertaken in addition to Musketry and Company drill.

2. Miscellaneous

There is nothing to add to the remarks contained in the statement for November 1914.

J. W. Payne
Major

War diaries of
2/7th Sherwood Foresters.

January to April
and
September to November
1915.

Volume No. _____

BRITISH SALONIKA FORCE

WAR DIARY.

M.T. Units with Serbian Army.

Vol. No.	Unit	PERIOD From	To
23.	Headquarters M.T. Units	1. 5. 18.	31. 5. 18.
22	688th M.T. Coy. ASC	1. 5. 18.	31. 5. 18.
12	689th M.T. Coy. A.S.C.	1. 5. 18	31. 5. 18.
16.	706th M.T. Coy. ASC	1. 5. 18.	31. 5. 18.
22.	707th M.T. Coy. ASC	1. 4. 18.	30. 4. 18.
19.	708th M.T. Coy. ASC	1. 5. 18.	31. 5. 18.
17	709 do.	1. 4. 18	30. 4. 18
18.	709 do	1. 5. 18	31. 5. 18
11.	819th M.T. Coy. ASC	1. 5. 18	31. 5. 18
11.	820th M.T. Coy. A.S.C.	1. 5. 18.	31. 5. 18.
10.	880th M.T. Coy. ASC	1. 5. 18.	31. 5. 18.
7.	881st M.T. Coy. A.S.C.	1. 5. 18.	31. 5. 18.

143 Bell

misc files

February

1917

Enfield

Army Form C. 2118

2/7th Sherwood Foresters

WAR DIARY
or
INTELLIGENCE SUMMARY.
(Erase heading not required.)

Instructions regarding War Diaries and Intelligence Summaries are contained in F.S. Regs., Part II. and the Staff Manual respectively. Title Pages will be prepared in manuscript.

Place	Date	Hour	Summary of Events and Information	Remarks and references to Appendices
NOTTINGHAM	2.1.15		The Battalion was inspected by Lieut. Gen. Sir R. Pole Carew KCB CVO on the Nottingham Forest Recreation Ground. The Inspector Officer expressed his satisfaction with the appearance of the Battalion & Major P.M. Payne who was in command.	
	13.1.15		The Double Company system was in to-day use.	
	15.1.15		The following orders of the new double Companies were appointed vz. A Co. - Capt W.S. Machell. B Co. Capt H.F. Hanson; C Co. Capt J. Rayner. J Co. ? Capt H.M. Whitehead. 2/Lt P.J. White was transferred to 8.M.R. Division Cyclist Co. 2/Lt's Hartle and Leut S.O. Pollard are under the duties of Lewis Machi? will expect from 30.11.14	
	16.1.15		The Battalion was inspected by Col. S. Ward Bannor Commanding the N.M. & Derby (Reserve) Infantry Brigade.	
	20.1.15		Lieut O.J. Porter was appointed Machine Gun Officer. The Machine Gun and Transport Sections were in any made	
	31.1.15		The Battalion was warned to proceed to its War Station at Luton on the following day. Mar. Rolls Strength Jan 1 - Officers 15 Men Rolls Jan 31 - 19	

Confidential

Statement for Jan. 1915.

2/7th Sherwood Foresters

1. Training

The training received by the Battalion during this month consisted of Platoon and Company drill, with occasional simple Tactical exercises by companies or two companies in conjunction. Each Company also dug its first set of trenches in Wollaton Park Notts. The soil was sandy and digging was easy.

2. Remounts

Horses were supplied to Mounted Officers during this month. They were small and generally speaking not of a stamp suitable for riding.

3. Miscellaneous

There is nothing to add to the remarks in last month.

J. Raynes. Captain
for Major Commanding 2/7
Sherwood Foresters

Army Form C. 2118

WAR DIARY
or
INTELLIGENCE SUMMARY
(Erase heading not required.)

2/7th Sherwood Foresters

Place	Date	Hour	Summary of Events and Information	Remarks and references to Appendices
Luton	Feb. 1915 1st		The Battalion moved up to Luton Station, Luton, where it was billeted in private billets at the 9d rate	YES
	6th		The name of the Battalion was changed to 2/7th Sherwood Foresters	YES
Luton	8th		The Battalion moved to Dijon to do trenches. Lieut. Col. G.A. Wigley took over the Command from Major P.M. Payne 7th Batt.	YES
	18th		In private houses at the 9d rate was received. The Battalion which then consisted of men who had joined since the war was added to the Home Service men then at Dijon – in number 185.	YES
			4 1/2 Cos. and men were sent as a draft to the 1/7th Sherwood Foresters at Braxley. These were all men who for various reasons had not proceeded with the 1/5th Battalion.	YES
	21st		2/7th given orders to proceed to join the 1/5th Battalion. The Battalion moved to Luton where it went into billets at the same area, at the same rate as before.	YES

Sheet 1. Feb. 1st/Mar. 28
O.M. Partlett 1196

Feb 28 March 22
J. M. Bayne
Major

Confidential 2/7th Sherwood Foresters
Statement with War Diary
February 1915

1. **Training** At Dyan consisted of digging trenches for the defence of London. At Luton Platoon, Company and Battalion drill and Route Marches.

2. **Billets** These were good and clean. It was found that by having all the billets together in streets parallel with one another and separated by single blocks of dwellings supervision was easy. At Dyan billets were at great distances apart, rendering supervision difficult.

3. **Discipline** Improvement in discipline was noticed directly the men left Nottingham and the environment of their homes.

4. **Medical Service** During the fortnight the Battalion was at Dyan, a medical officer was temporarily attached. The health of the men was not good then as their work was carried on under most unfavourable conditions. They were frequently ankle deep in water during their trenching operations.

5. **Arms** The Japanese rifles with which the Battalion was issued were useless with which to teach the actions of loading and unloading. No dummy ammunition was available; and the projecting platforms made it impossible to close the bolt smartly

J M Dayrell Major

Army Form C. 2118

WAR DIARY
or
INTELLIGENCE SUMMARY
(Erase heading not required.)

2/7 Th Manchester

Place	Date	Hour	Summary of Events and Information	Remarks and references to Appendices
Lulu	March 1915			
	2		The Battalion took part in a Brigade Inspection by General Sir Ian Hamilton G.C.B. K.C.B. GOC i/c Central Force.	JMD
	3		The Battalion was inspected by Brigadier General Nelles C.B. in Stockwood Park Luton	JMD
	4		Men were posted to the Batt. from 1/5 th Batt.	JMD
	8		Two Japanese Rifle Coys given to 200 men of H Co.	JMD
	16		3½ 2COs and men transferred to Base details.	JMD
	22		A fresh C/o was received by the Battalion. 16 men transferred from Base details to the Battalion.	JMD
	24		150 men were transferred to the 3/7 G Battalion. Men were received by the Battalion	JMD
	30		32 Heavy draft men were received by the Battalion.	JMD
			Strength March 1915: 22 OR 1134
			March 31: 33 " 1064

J. M. Dayrell
Major

Confidential

7/7th Sherwood Foresters.
Statement with War Diary
March 1915.

———

1. <u>Training</u> consisted of Battalion Company and Platoon drill with Route Marches and tactical exercises.

2. <u>Medical Service</u> As this battalion had no medical officer attached to it, the Medical Officers of the 6th and 8th Battalions shared the work between them.

3. <u>Remounts</u>:- The 9 pack cobs and 32 draught horses supplied were satisfactory.

J. M. Dalrymple
Major

Army Form C. 2118

WAR DIARY
or
INTELLIGENCE SUMMARY 37th Glenwock Fuseliers
(Erase heading not required.)

Instructions regarding War Diaries and Intelligence Summaries are contained in F. S. Regs., Part II. and the Staff Manual respectively. Title Pages will be prepared in manuscript.

Place	Date	Hour	Summary of Events and Information	Remarks and references to Appendices
Luli	April 1915		2nd Lieut. J. G. Strahan proceeded overseas to join the expeditionary force.	Yes
			Nothing of note occurred during the month.	Yes

Strength April 1 Officers 36 OR 1097
              30   39   1086

S. V. Sayer
Major

Confidential 2/7th Sherwood Foresters

Statement with War Diary
April 1915.

1. Training as before with the addition of Night Work.

2. Miscellaneous all other matters as for March 1915.

J. M. Dalrymple

CONFIDENTIAL.

Army Form C. 2118

WAR DIARY

or

INTELLIGENCE SUMMARY

(Erase heading not required.)

2/7TH BATTALION, SHERWOOD FORESTERS.

Instructions regarding War Diaries and Intelligence Summaries are contained in F. S. Regs., Part II. and the Staff Manual respectively. Title Pages will be prepared in manuscript.

Place	Date	Hour	Summary of Events and Information	Remarks and references to Appendices
WATFORD	2/9/15.		Company Serjt-Major Pope was tried by District Court Martial for conduct prejudicial to good order and discipline.	7cd
	3/9/15.		2/Lieuts. P.W. Mellor, P.C. Perry, F.P. Sims, and E.R. Barlow reported for duty from the 3/7th Battalion.	7cd
	5/9/15.		Corporal Baggaley and Private Nicholson were tried by District Court Martial for conduct prejudicial to discipline and drunkenness on duty respectively. Company Serjt-Major Pope reduced to Serjt by D.C.M. held on 2.9.15 and the Sentence promulgated.	7cd
	7/9/15.		The Right Hon.The Earl of Essex visited the Camp.	7cd
	15/9/15.		The 59th (N.M.) Division was inspected by the G.O.C. 2/Lieut. R.W. Hoyte reported for duty.	7cd
	20/9/15.		Lieut. E.P. Satchell, R.A.M.C., reported for duty as Medical Officer.	7cd
	24/9/15.		2/Lieut. R.B. Emmett reported for duty.	7cd
			STRENGTH { Septr. 1st 19 Officers 702 Other ranks. Septr. 30th. 26 : 700 :	7cd

J.M.Dayull
Major,

Confidential

Army Form C. 2118.

WAR=DIARY
or
INTELLIGENCE SUMMARY.

(*Erase heading not required.*)

2/7th BATTALION, SHERWOOD FORESTERS.

Instructions regarding War Diaries and Intelligence Summaries are contained in F. S. Regs., Part II. and the Staff Manual respectively. Title pages will be prepared in manuscript.

Hour, Date, Place	Summary of Events and Information	Remarks and references to Appendices
WATFORD, September 1915.	1. TRAINING. ------ Brigade Field days were undertaken: also Battalion Field Days over defined large areas. 2. ORDNANCE. ------ Field Kitchens were supplied and worked satisfactorily. They were taken out on FIELD OPERATIONS and other long days. It was found that the type of draught horse which had been issued was not heavy enough for these Vehicles. 3. REMOUNTS. ------ See No.2. 4. MEDICAL SERVICE. ------ Up to this month, the 2/7th Battalion had had the Services of the Medical Officers of the 2/6th and 2/8th Battalions.	

L M Payne
Major

Army Form C. 2118

WAR DIARY
or
INTELLIGENCE SUMMARY
(Erase heading not required.)

2/7th Sherwood Foresters.

Instructions regarding War Diaries and Intelligence Summaries are contained in F.S. Regs., Part II. and the Staff Manual respectively. Title Pages will be prepared in manuscript.

Place	Date	Hour	Summary of Events and Information	Remarks and references to Appendices
WATFORD.	1/10/15.		The Battalion took part in an inspection of the 59th (North Midland) Division by General Sir Leslie Rundle, G.C.B., G.C.M.G., G.C.V.O., D.S.O., G.O.C. Central Force in GORHAMBURY PARK. 2nd. Lieutenants F.G.Henry, J.Macpherson, F.C.Dietrichsen, F.Pragnell and C.F.Maltby promoted to be Lieutenants as from 16. 8. 15.	
	5/10/15.		Divisional Field Day.	
	18th		The Battalion removed from Camp to Billets in WATFORD.	
	22nd.		Captain H.Hanson returned to duty from Divisional Headquarters. 2nd Lieutenant Claude Frederick Parry reported for duty.	
	26th.		Lieutenants W.F.Player, and J.Macpherson; and 2nd Lieutenants F.P.Sims, E.R.Barlow and R.B.Emmett proceeded overseas to join the Expeditionary Force.	
			STRENGTH. October 1. Officers. 26. Other Ranks. 699. October 31st. Officers. 21. Other Ranks. 697.	

H.Hanson Capt.
for Major
Commanding 2/7 Batt.
Sherwood Foresters

Army Form C. 2118

WAR=DIARY
or
INTELLIGENCE SUMMARY
(Erase heading not required.)

Instructions regarding War Diaries and Intelligence Summaries are contained in F.S. Regs., Part II. and the Staff Manual respectively. Title Pages will be prepared in manuscript.

Place	Date	Hour	Summary of Events and Information	Remarks and references to Appendices
WATFORD.	Oct r 1915.		1. TRAINING. Divisional Operations were undertaken in conjunction with the rest of the Division. 2. BILLETING. The men were at first Billeted in private houses, Messing Centrally. The accommodation was very limited, with the consequence that the men were not so comfortable as they had been when messing in their billets. Later, two Companies were removed into a School, and an extra Mess-room was obtained. 3. ORDNANCE. 75 out of a total of 600 Japanese Rifles were withdrawn.	

H. Harrison
Capt
for Major
Commanding 2/7 Bn Warwick Territorials

Army Form C. 2118

2/7 Sherwood Foresters

WAR DIARY
or
INTELLIGENCE SUMMARY
(Erase heading not required.)

Instructions regarding War Diaries and Intelligence Summaries are contained in F.S. Regs., Part II. and the Staff Manual respectively. Title Pages will be prepared in manuscript.

Place	Date	Hour	Summary of Events and Information	Remarks and references to Appendices
WATFORD	November 1915			
	1st		Strength Officers 21 Other Ranks 698 including attached	
	3rd		The Battalion took part in Brigade Field Operations.	
	6th		67 NCOs & men were transferred to the 29th Provisional Battalion for Home Service, but the transfer was postponed	
	9th		The Battalion took part in Divisional Operations	
	10th		The Battalion was inspected by Maj. Gen. C.T. Dixon, Inspector of Infantry in Moore Park	
	13th		Major General R.A.R. Renser C.B. took over the command of the Division	
	16th		The G.O.C. 59th (2nd N.) Division inspected the Battalion	
	17th		67 NCOs and men were transferred to the 29th Provincial Battalion.	
	19th		It was published in Battalion Orders that 2nd Lieut (Temporary Captain) C.E. Vickers 1/7th Sherwood Foresters had been awarded the Victoria Cross for most conspicuous bravery on October 14th 1915. N.B. The Hohenzollern Redoubt. This Officer served with the 2/7th Sherwood Foresters from 2nd September until 10.11.14: Also Hon. Lieut (Temporary Captain) J.H. Browne 2/7th Sherwood Foresters	

Army Form C. 2118.

2/7 Th Sherwood Foresters

WAR DIARY
or
INTELLIGENCE SUMMARY.
(Erase heading not required.)

Instructions regarding War Diaries and Intelligence Summaries are contained in F. S. Regs., Part II. and the Staff Manual respectively. Title pages will be prepared in manuscript.

Hour, Date, Place	Summary of Events and Information	Remarks and References to Appendices

WATFORD
November 1915.
19th — Cpt. J. West was awarded the Military Gen. for conspicuous gallantry at Hargicourt October 13th 1915.

23rd — A Brigade chapter took place in Moor Park before the G.O.C. 59th (2.N.) Division.

25th — A divisional Route March took place in which the Batt. when active to part of the Field Column.

29th — Company Training commenced. A and C Companies were the first to undertake it.

30th — Kensal. Major J. Mason 21 the Rank C 627 R.B. during the month 2 R.E.O.S. were transferred to the Battalions, and 5 men to the Royal Flying Corps.

M. Raynor
Major

Forms/C. 2118/10.

Statement attached to War Diary
for November 1915.
2/7th Sherwood Foresters.

1. **Billeting**. Two companies were in private billets and two were billeted in a large School - Chalet School. The latter were very satisfactorily housed, the men being all together with consequent easy supervision, and the building being very well adapted for the purpose.

Numerous schemes were suggested for billeting the other two Companies in empty houses instead of private billets, no large houses being available. They were unsatisfactory from every point of view. The men being separated over a wide area, small parties in each house, would be difficult to supervise; and all the houses selected were at a very considerable distance from the Central messing halls - in some cases half a mile - which would make the consumption of meals in the time allotted impossible, if the men were to have any adequate rest.

2. **Messing**.
Messing was central, two companies messing in one hall, two in another. This arrangement would have been quite satisfactory, had proper barrack furniture been supplied

2. Messing Continued

but being constrained to use chairs instead of forms, and very wide tables, it was found that far too much room was occupied, and it was impossible to move with any comfort. Barrack furniture for the men's rooms is an urgent necessity.

3. Band

The Regimental Band, the instruments of which had been presented privately, was broken up and disbanded. The Band had acquired a high degree of excellence during the few months it had been in existence; the men were proud of it, and it was a great disappointment to officers and men when it had to be disbanded.

The Band accompanying the Battalion was a great attraction to the Civilian population and to some extent was an incentive to recruiting.

4. Horses

The officers riding horses originally issued to the Battalion were not a good stamp of riding horses, being evidently driving cobs, small and in many cases not up to carrying a man for any length of time. During this month, after nearly twelve months service, it has become clear that most of them are unsuited for the work they have to do

Army Form C. 2118

WAR DIARY
or
INTELLIGENCE SUMMARY
(Erase heading not required.)

7/7th [illegible] Force "A"

Instructions regarding War Diaries and Intelligence Summaries are contained in F.S. Regs., Part II. and the Staff Manual respectively. Title Pages will be prepared in manuscript.

Place	Date	Hour	Summary of Events and Information	Remarks and references to Appendices
Watful	Dec 1915 2		4 men transferred from 30th Divn.	
	3		1 man struck off the strength as a recruit	
			No 3647 Pte H Rollley sentenced to 42 days detention by a Regimental Court Martial	
	7th		1 man struck off the strength on recruit	
	8th		1 man discharged on appointment to a commission in the 14th Res. Batt. Rifle Brigade	
	9th		17 CO transferred to 29 to Provisional Battn.	
	10th		13 men transferred to 29th Provisional Battn.	
	11th		12 men struck off the strength as a Recruits	
	13		12 men	
	17th		12 men discharged with RK 392(6)	
	16th		No 1834 Pte H Gallan sentenced to 90 days detention by DCM to desertion	
	22		1 man taken on the strength having been noted as a deserter	
	26th		Capt JG Henry appointed B.M.G.O.	
	31st		No 3314 Pte Benj Mitchell sentenced to 30 days detention in absence by R.C.M.	
			Strength Dec 1. Officers 21 O.R. 624 Dec 31 Officers 21 O.R. 626	

P McDayal Major

Statement attached to War Diary
for December 1915 2/7th Sherwood
Foresters

Watford 1. Billets: During this month nine men were quartered in empty houses. Considerable difficulty and delay has been experienced in obtaining barrack furniture. Proper Barrack tables are an urgent necessity as those in use, consisting merely of boards on trestles are far too wide for their purpose, and being open-jointed are difficult to keep clean.

2. Messing: It is possible now at the end of the year to draw a comparison between purchasing stores through a contractor, and purchasing in the open market regimentally. The balance of advantage is in favour of the latter method. In many instances it was found, when purchasing through a contractor that goods were delivered to stores straight from merchants in the town, without passing through the contractor's hands at all, and that the price being paid for such goods was 20% higher than than what would have been charged by the merchant, had they been bought direct: and indeed 20% higher than what was actually paid after the system of purchasing regimentally had been substituted for that of purchasing through a contractor.

Messing Continued

It has been found that the greater the experience of the Institution of Central Messing, the more can be done for the comfort of the men. The Battalion under my command got a very good report from the Inspector of Messing; but every day sees some improvement introduced into the system.

3. Discipline

In cases of absence without leave I introduced the plan of trying old offenders by R.C.M. The sentences given by these courts were very much longer than I could give under KR 493(1), and the result was that this offence decreased in frequency.

4. Company Training

In accordance with Divisional Orders, Company training was undergone and proved very beneficial to Officers, NCOs and men. The greatest difficulty experienced was to replace employed men, e.g. cooks and transport men withdrawn for training. Those temporarily so employed were quite new to their duties, and required constant supervision.

P. W. Payne
Major

Subject:- War Diary.

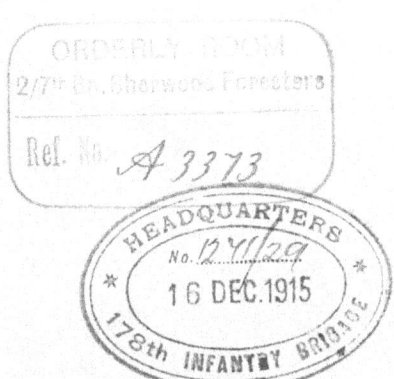

From O.C.
    2/7th Sherwood Foresters

To Headquarters
    178th Infantry Brigade.

                  Reference your letter No.1271/29 of 15/12/15.

                  The number are as follows:-

Total Numbers who left the Battalion.	83.
Transferred to other Battalions.	9.
Transferred to 29th Provisional Battalion.	69.
Struck off as a Deserter.	1.
Discharged on obtaining Commissions.	3.
Discharged under Para:392 6 (a) K.R.	1.

Watford,
16/12/15.

                        Major,
Commanding 2/7th Sherwood Foresters.

From :- O.C.,
       2/7th Sherwood Foresters.

To   :- Headquarters,
        178th Infantry Brigade,
        Watford.

WAR DIARIES.

With reference to your Circular letter No.1271/29 of 25/10/15.

On going into this matter, I find that the late Orderly Room Sergeant, who was transferred to the 29th Provisional Battalion in June last, destroyed the file copies of the Regimental Daily Orders from the date of formation to December 31st, 1915. There are not, therefore, in this Office at the present time, any papers from which necessary information for the War Diary could be obtained.

Some days ago, I wrote to the Officer in Charge Territorial Force Records, Lichfield, asking him to supply me with certain information to enable me to prepare the War Diary up to the end of last year. As soon as I receive this information, I will prepare the Diary and send it on.

Watford,
27/10/15.

Major,
Commanding 2/7th Sherwood Foresters.

Subject:- War Diary.

From:- O.C. 2/6th Bn. The Sherwood Foresters.
To:- Headquarters, 178th Infantry Brigade.

WATFORD,
15th Dec. 1915.

With reference to your letter 1271/29 dated 15th inst. I beg to state below the details required,-

3rd Nov./15. 29 men to 29th Provisional Battn.
4th "   "   1 man Discharged.
8th "   "   1 man transferred from 3/6th Bn.S.F.
17th "   "   4 men to 29th Provisional Battn.

Lieut.Col.
Cdg.2/6th Bn. The Sherwood Foresters.

Confidential

War Diary

of

2/7th Batt. Sherwood Foresters

From 1st to 31st January 1916

Volume XVI

Confidential

Army Form C. 2118

WAR DIARY
or
INTELLIGENCE SUMMARY
2/7th Sherwood Foresters

(Erase heading not required.)

Instructions regarding War Diaries and Intelligence Summaries are contained in F.S. Regs., Part II. and the Staff Manual respectively. Title Pages will be prepared in manuscript.

Place	Date	Hour	Summary of Events and Information	Remarks and references to Appendices
Watford	Jan 1916			
	5	5 pm	Pte 3747 Pte W. Butler sentenced 42 days detention by Lt Col C.R.	JC0
	7	7 pm	3 men discharged under para 392 K.R.	JC0
		10	1 man transferred to 29th Provisional Batt at Wareham	JC0
	14			JC0
		3 pm	1 man transferred to 2/1st N. Mid R.F.A.	JC0
	23		24 men Army Reserve called up and joined the Battalion	JC0
		10	" " " " " "	JC0
	24	15	" " " " " "	JC0
		10	" " " " " "	JC0
	26	17	" " " " " "	JC0
	27	7	" " " " " "	JC0
	28	12	" " " " " "	JC0
			No 2953 Private S. Cooper sentenced to 3 months detention by L.Col.	JC9
	29	13	men Army Reserve called up and joined the Batt.	JC8
	30	26	" " " " " "	JC8
	31	7	" " " " " "	JC0
			Strength Jan 1 Officers 31 OR 625	
			" Jan 31 " 23 " 737.	

P.V. Vosough
Major

2/7th Sherwood Foresters
Statement with War Diary
Jan 1916.

Confidential

1. <u>Training</u> consisted of general training as before for two companies, while two other Companies underwent Special Company training. This proved most beneficial to the Companies concerned.

2. <u>Recruits</u> The Derby Recruits are of a moderate stamp physically, but being young, will probably quickly respond to training. Mentally they are of a superior standard and shew already the results of a few days' drill and instruction.

3. <u>Miscellaneous</u> There is nothing to add to my remarks for December 1915

J. M. Payne

Confidential

War Diary

of

2/7th Sherwood Foresters

From Feb 1st 1916 to Feb 29th 1916

(V.I. XVII)

Army Form C. 2118

WAR DIARY
or
INTELLIGENCE SUMMARY
(Erase heading not required.)

Instructions regarding War Diaries and Intelligence Summaries are contained in F. S. Regs., Part II. and the Staff Manual respectively. Title Pages will be prepared in manuscript.

Place	Date 1916	Hour	Summary of Events and Information	Remarks and references to Appendices
WATFORD	Feb.	2	16 men of Army Reserve joined the Battalion	JCo
		3	9 " " " " " "	JCo
		5	8 " " " " " "	JCo
		6	16 " " " " " "	JCo
		7	13 " " " " " "	JCo
		10	20 " " " " " "	Jco
		11	20 " " " " " "	JCo
		12	13 " " " " " "	JCo
		13	7 " " " " " "	
		14	40 " " " " " "	JCo
		19	1 man transferred to Royal Engineers	JCo
		21	Lt Col C Fane DSO took over the Command of the Battalion vice Major Parr TD	JCo
		22	1 N.C.O. discharged to Commission of engagement	JCo
		23	1 man transferred to Queens R.W.R	JCo
		26	1 man transferred to R.E.	JCo
		28	1 man transferred to Royal West Kent	JCo

Sheet 17 pict. 1st March 23 TR 737
24 OR 959

W.O. Staff H.Q.
2/7 Glouer Gazette

1875. Wt. W 593/826 1,000,000 4/15 J.R.C. & A. A.D.S.S./Forms/C. 2118.

Confidential

2/7th Battalion
The Sherwood Foresters

Statement with War Diary for
Feb. 1916

There is nothing to add to
the Statement for January 1916

28-2-16

Cecil Fane Lt Col
2/7 Sherwood Foresters

www.ingramcontent.com/pod-product-compliance
Lightning Source LLC
Chambersburg PA
CBHW081458160426
43193CB00013B/2527